Hal•Leonard
Instrumental Play-Along

FLUTE

MOTOWN CLASSICS

T0039514

How To Use The CD Accompaniment:

A melody cue appears on the right channel only.
If your CD player has a balance adjustment, you can adjust the volume
of the melody by turning down the right channel.

The CD is playable on any CD player, and is also enhanced so Mac and PC users
can adjust the recording to any tempo without changing the pitch!

ISBN: 978-1-4584-0556-2

HAL•LEONARD®
CORPORATION

7777 W. BLUEMOUND RD. P.O. BOX 13819 MILWAUKEE, WI 53213

Visit Hal Leonard Online at
www.halleonard.com

CONTENTS

	PAGE	CD TRACK
ABC THE JACKSON 5	4	1
AIN'T NO MOUNTAIN HIGH ENOUGH DIANA ROSS	6	2
BABY LOVE THE SUPREMES	7	3
ENDLESS LOVE DIANA ROSS & LIONEL RICHIE	8	4
HOW SWEET IT IS (TO BE LOVED BY YOU) MARVIN GAYE	10	5
I CAN'T HELP MYSELF (SUGAR PIE, HONEY BUNCH) THE FOUR TOPS	12	6
I JUST CALLED TO SAY I LOVE YOU STEVIE WONDER	14	7
I'LL BE THERE THE JACKSON 5	15	8
MY CHERIE AMOUR STEVIE WONDER	16	9
MY GIRL THE TEMPTATIONS	18	11
STOP! IN THE NAME OF LOVE THE SUPREMES	20	12
THREE TIMES A LADY THE COMMODORES	17	10
THE TRACKS OF MY TEARS THE MIRACLES	22	13
WHAT'S GOING ON MARVIN GAYE	23	14
YOU'VE REALLY GOT A HOLD ON ME THE MIRACLES	24	15
B♭ TUNING NOTES		16

◆ ABC

FLUTE

Words and Music by ALPHONSO MIZELL,
FREDERICK PERREN, DEKE RICHARDS
and BERRY GORDY

5

❷ AIN'T NO MOUNTAIN HIGH ENOUGH

FLUTE

Words and Music by NICKOLAS ASHFORD
and VALERIE SIMPSON

❸ BABY LOVE

Flute

Words and Music by BRIAN HOLLAND,
EDWARD HOLLAND and LAMONT DOZIER

◆ ENDLESS LOVE

FLUTE

Words and Music by
LIONEL RICHIE

HOW SWEET IT IS
(To Be Loved by You)

Flute

Words and Music by EDWARD HOLLAND,
LAMONT DOZIER and BRIAN HOLLAND

◆ I CAN'T HELP MYSELF
(Sugar Pie, Honey Bunch)

FLUTE

Words and Music by BRIAN HOLLAND,
LAMONT DOZIER and EDWARD HOLLAND

◆7 I JUST CALLED TO SAY I LOVE YOU

Flute

Words and Music by
STEVIE WONDER

8 I'LL BE THERE

Flute

Words and Music by BERRY GORDY,
HAL DAVIS, WILLIE HUTCH
and BOB WEST

◆ 9 MY CHERIE AMOUR

Flute

Words and Music by STEVIE WONDER,
SYLVIA MOY and HENRY COSBY

◆10 THREE TIMES A LADY

Flute

Words and Music by
LIONEL RICHIE

⓫ MY GIRL

FLUTE

Words and Music by WILLIAM "SMOKEY" ROBINSON
and RONALD WHITE

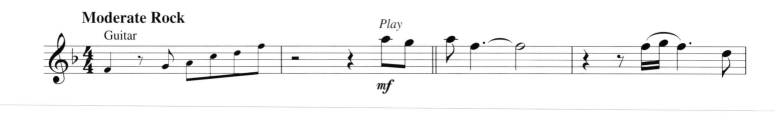

◆⟨12⟩ STOP! IN THE NAME OF LOVE

FLUTE

Words and Music by LAMONT DOZIER,
BRIAN HOLLAND and EDWARD HOLLAND

◆13 THE TRACKS OF MY TEARS

FLUTE

Words and Music by WILLIAM "SMOKEY" ROBINSON,
WARREN MOORE and MARVIN TARPLIN

Moderately, with feeling

◆ WHAT'S GOING ON

Flute

Words and Music by RENALDO BENSON,
ALFRED CLEVELAND and MARVIN GAYE

⬥ YOU'VE REALLY GOT A HOLD ON ME

Flute

Words and Music by
WILLIAM "SMOKEY" ROBINSON